First

Expert Pet Care

CARING
for
Dogs

by Tammy Gagne

Raintree is an imprint of Capstone Global Library Limited, a company incorporated in
England and Wales having its registered office at 264 Banbury Road, Oxford, OX2 7DY –
Registered company number: 6695582

www.raintree.co.uk
myorders@raintree.co.uk

Edited by Marissa Kirkman
Designed by Sarah Bennett
Original illustrations © Capstone Global Library Limited 2019
Picture research by Tracy Cummins
Production by Laura Manthe
Originated by Capstone Global Library Ltd
Printed and bound in India

ISBN 978 1 4747 6086 7
22 21 20 19 18
10 9 8 7 6 5 4 3 2 1

**British Library Cataloguing in Publication Data**
A full catalogue record for this book is available from the British Library.

**Acknowledgements**
We would like to thank the following for permission to reproduce photographs: iStockphoto:
kali9, 9, 10, tdub303, 15; Shutterstock: anetapics, 19, ANURAK PONGPATIMET, 6 (bed),
ARTSILENSE, 24, Asia Images Group, 12, BIGANDT.COM, 21 Middle Right, Cynthia Valdez,
7, Darren Baker, 13, Dora Zett, 4, 21 Bottom, ekmelica, Design Element, Elayne Massaini, 21
Middle Left, Eric Isselee, Cover, Back Cover, 3, gpointstudio, 17, Grigorita Ko, 16, hd connelly,
6 (toys), Igor Normann, 18, maksimee, 6 (bowls), Martin Maun, 20, Moolkum, 6 (brush), Nicole
Lienemann, 11, Okssi, 6 (leash), Roland IJdema, 21 Top, Susan Schmitz, 23, unguryanu, 5,
vvvita, 8.

# Contents

# Your new pet dog

Are you looking for a pet you can run and play with outside? A dog may be the perfect pet for you. Dogs and their owners can do many things together. Many dogs in need of homes are in **shelters**.

Owning a dog is a **responsibility**, and you need to be prepared. There is much to learn before bringing your dog home.

There are many types of dogs. Your family will need to decide which type of dog is right for your home.

**shelter** place that takes care of, and rehomes, lost or stray animals

**responsibility** duty or a job

# Things you will need

Every dog needs bowls for food and water. Dogs should also have a few toys. Toys help to stop them chewing things they shouldn't.

Your dog will also need a bed, brush and lead. Leads attach to either a collar or a harness. ID tags and **microchips** will help if your dog is ever lost. They show people who the dog belongs to and how to contact the owner.

**microchip** tiny device that stores information about an animal, such as its owner's name and address

**FACT**

Use a harness instead of a collar to teach your dog how to walk properly on the lead. It is easier to control a dog's movement with a harness.

# Bringing your pet home

Your new dog may be tired or scared when you bring it home. Limit meetings to just your family for the first day. Use care when your dog meets other pets. Even friendly dogs can hurt cats or other small animals.

Start **house-training** your dog straight away. Puppies may have accidents until they learn where they should go to the toilet.

Always introduce your dog to new people and animals slowly. Rushing can make your pet feel stressed.

**house-train** teach a pet where to go to the toilet

# Food gives dogs energy

Adult dogs should eat twice a day. Owners may feed them dry or wet food. Your **vet** can advise you on the best type of food for your dog.

Puppies need special food made for their growing bodies. Because their stomachs are so small, they will need to eat three meals each day.

**vet** doctor trained to take care of animals

**FACT**

Dogs love getting treats. But too many treats can make a dog gain too much weight.

# Keeping clean

Dogs with long or thick hair need to be brushed and bathed regularly. Even short-haired dogs that spend lots of time outside may also need more **grooming**.

It is important to clear up your dog's poo. You should always take bags with you on a walk. Use them to scoop up the poo and throw it in a dog waste bin.

Never use your shampoo on your dog. Dogs need special shampoo that is made for them.

**grooming** washing and brushing an animal

# Check-up time

Even healthy dogs should visit a vet once a year. Vets can give advice about feeding, grooming and **training**. Dogs need to have medicines to **prevent** diseases and protect them from fleas.

Your dog can be **spayed** or **neutered** when it is six months old. This stops dogs from having puppies.

**FACT**

You can keep your dog calm at the vet by stroking it gently. You can also take a treat or two along with you.

**training** learning and practising new skills

**prevent** stop something from happening

**spay** operate on a female animal so it is unable to produce young

**neuter** operate on a male animal so it is unable to produce young

# Life with a dog

There are lots of new skills you can teach your dog. You can teach your dog to "sit" and "stay". Some dogs even learn tricks such as "roll over" and "fetch".

It is also important to give your dog plenty of playtime. Playing gives your pet exercise. This helps keep its body healthy. Games such as fetch and hide-and-seek also exercise your pet's mind.

Being the seeker in a game of hide-and-seek, will help to teach your dog to come to you.

# Your dog through the years

Your dog will have more energy while it is young. Older dogs are calmer and like to sleep more.

Some dogs have longer **life spans** than others. Most dogs live for at least 10 years. Some even live to be 15 or older. As an owner, try to make every day with your dog the best it can be.

**life span** number of years a certain type of plant or animal usually lives

# Dog body language

How a dog behaves tells us a lot about what it is feeling. Tail wagging often means a dog is happy. Growling is a sign the dog is angry. A dog that raises its nose into the air may sense another person or animal nearby.

# Types of dogs

Some of the most active dogs are:

- Golden retrievers
- Labrador retrievers
- Siberian huskies.

Labrador retriever

Border collie

Siberian husky

German shepherd

The cleverest dogs include:

- Border collies
- German shepherds
- Poodles.

21

# Glossary

**grooming**  washing and brushing an animal

**house-train**  teach a pet where to go to the toilet

**life span**  number of years a certain type of plant or animal usually lives

**microchip**  tiny device that stores information about an animal, such as its owner's name and address

**neuter**  operate on a male animal so it is unable to produce young

**prevent**  stop something from happening

**responsibility**  duty or job

**shelter**  place that takes care of, and rehomes, lost or stray animals

**spay**  operate on a female animal so it is unable to produce young

**training**  learning and practising new skills

**vet**  doctor trained to take care of animals

# Find out more

## Books

*Caring for Dogs and Puppies* (Battersea Dogs and Cats Home: Pet Care Guides), Ben Hubbard (Franklin Watts, 2015)

*Dogs: Facts at Your Fingertips* (Pocket Eyewitness), DK (DK Children, 2018)

*Looking After Dogs and Puppies* (Pet Guides), Katherine Starke (Usborne, 2013)

*Ruff's Guide to Caring for Your Dog* (Pets' Guides), Anita Ganeri (Raintree, 2014)

*The Truth About Dogs: What Dogs Do When You're Not Looking* (Pets Undercover!), Mary Colson (Raintree, 2018)

## Websites

Find out more about pet care at
**www.dkfindout.com/uk/animals-and-nature/pet-care**

Learn more about all sorts of animals and how to take care of them at:
**young.rspca.org.uk/kids/animals**

# Comprehension questions

1. What things will you need to buy for your dog?
2. How often will you need to feed your dog?
3. What types of games can you play with your dog?

# Index